Great Leaps

in a
Single Bound

Käaren Witte

BETHANY HOUSE PUBLISHERS
MINNEAPOLIS, MN 55438

Copyright © 1982
Käaren Witte

Published by Bethany House Publishers
A Division of Bethany Fellowship, Inc.
6820 Auto Club Road, Minneapolis, Minnesota 55438

Printed in the United States of America

Library of Congress Cataloging in Publication Data

Witte, Käaren.
   Great leaps in a single bound.

    1. Single women—Religious life.
2. Witte, Käaren. I. Title.
BV4596.S5W57   248.8'432   82-4163
ISBN 0-87123-199-9 (pbk.)   AACR2

Dedication

TO DAD, Al Witte:

> Who gave me roots and wings.
> Because of his love, I can just begin to understand the love of God.

TO MOM, Lilly Nelson Witte:

> Who told me to tell my generation that Jesus Christ is the reason to live, and the reason to die.

TO Mrs. Hazel Witte:

> The greatest answer to prayer in my life so far. She would have been my mom's best friend. I just know it. (They're both angels.) I'll call her Mom II.

About the Author

KÄAREN WITTE lives, when she's home, in Minneapolis, Minnesota. But a great slice of her life is spent on the road, traveling as speaker and teacher all across the nation. She is a veteran of both radio and TV, having produced her own "Years to Youth" series for WCCO-TV and hosted the "Truly Liberated Woman" series for the Northwestern Radio Network. She has been a news correspondent, a junior-high school teacher and a short-term missionary. She has appeared nationally on the PTL Club, the 700 Club, and Dr. Dobson's "Focus on the Family." This is her second book.

Acknowledgements

These are God's gifts to me. Friends. I wish you knew them. They know God.

I admire these men. They've listened to me and believed in me. They think I'm just keen. (They think like our Christ.): Dr. Leith Anderson, Pastor Doug Fagerstrom, Bruce Ribnick, Frank Masserano, Earl Fredrickson, Marc Seager, Rev. Robert Crumbley, "First Hand" Denny Milgate, Bill Reimer, Norm Plasch.

These are friends who regularly laugh with me, pray with me, and cry with me: Marie Johnson, Dee Ann Weitgenant Werner, Jaynee Harsma Tutt, Sandy Peterson, Vicki Radford, Marilyn Eerdmans, Jeanne Marie Crabtree, Cheryl Gibbons, Karen Luedtke, Pat Jensen, Mary Jo Dale, Ruthi Olson Anderson, Jan Markell, Cheryl Peterson, Catherine Jane Reishus, Carolyn Pearl Owens.

Also by Käaren Witte:
Angels in Faded Jeans

Introduction

I'm going to open my heart and let you walk around.

It's a risk.

Because, in my doing so, you will see my hurts, longings, mistakes, failures, and secrets.

I'll take that risk.

Because maybe, just maybe, you feel as I do. Maybe you'll taste the salt when the tears run down my face.

Maybe, too, you'll laugh with me. Praise with me. And pray with me. I'd like that.

I'll take the first risk by saying I need you. It's rather frightening to say that to the "me" generation—when cool, mellow, laidback, subtle people want to win through intimidation and pull their own strings.

Here's my heart. Come on in!

I'm single.

I have never been married.

I walk alone—in one sense—in this great adventure called Life.

Sometimes I laugh.

Sometimes I cry.

Sometimes I struggle with God.

Or try to manipulate Him.

I sit in the first row of my growing suburban church (and have for ten years).

I sit with two solid rows of other single young women—

Women like me—

Trusting, praying, believing God for a life's mate. His first choice.

I look at these women.

They are my friends.

They are warm and friendly, attractive and well-dressed.

Sometimes they wear a fresh-flower corsage earned by pouring punch at somebody else's wedding.

We've played volleyball and gone on retreats together,

sung hymns at singspirations and prayed together at meetings and Bible studies.

God has not chosen to give us the gift of a family, or children, or a husband—yet.

But we wait.

He is still a great God. And we believe that whatever He does, *He does in love*—

Even when we don't understand Him.

We listen to our pastor's messages: "Don't pray for a mate for someone. Just pray for God's glory in that life."

So we pray that way too. Believing, trusting.

(But sometimes we pray for a life's mate anyway.)

Jesus understands.

I just know it.

When I Was Eleven

We left Chicago for Minnesota.
My father had bought a small-town hotel.
    (That's a Chicagoland dream: A move to Minnesota.)
We lived in an apartment in the hotel.
But in a small town families live in houses with lawns, patios,
    and grills.
I didn't want to be different.
My mother once said that rich, privileged people lived in hotels.
    (It made me feel a little better.)
The hotel patrons were homeless men who read the newspa-
    per in the lobby, and lifted their feet without looking up
    when our washing machine overflowed and sent a streak of
    soapy water sliding over the tiled floor.
Once at the candy store, the lady clerk asked us where we
    lived.
My two little friends spouted their addresses.
When I told mine, she said, "That place has a bad reputa-
    tion."
I burned with humiliation.
I didn't know how to define it then.
And an eleven-year-old doesn't know how to defend such a
    remark or dismiss it.
You just hear it replayed.
For a long time afterward.

May 1964

The Senior Banquet

Banquet night. Not the junior banquet. The *senior* banquet. Everybody managed to find someone to take. Or go with.

I thought it was unfair. Even the guys with greasy hair who needed industrial-strength deodorant got girls to go with them for the senior banquet.

I listened to the high-pitched chatter from the girls, "Yipes! I'm going to sneak out of study hall early so I can get home and start getting ready!" one classmate wailed.

"You! I can't even get my hair done until 4:00 . . . that only leaves me two hours before Rich comes!" another yelled above the noise on her way out the door of the girls' washroom.

I just kept combing my hair. I couldn't join in their excitement. They didn't care. It was their parade. No one was about to "reach out" and make a girl feel good who wasn't a part of the gala. Not on this day, anyway. It was their day in the sun. Their chance at bat. Not mine.

I felt my cheeks burn. Did they guess that I was feeling rejected and humiliated? I panicked. How I hoped not!

"Get out of here! Quit combing your hair in rote!" I slapped myself mentally. I tossed different possibilities around in my head.

I could act like . . . *Oh, Big Deal*—the rinky-dink high-school banquet. *La-Dee-Da*. How provincial. Or, I could ask questions in awe about their glorious formals and the gorgeous guys they were going with.

"Forget it! Leave! Walk through the laughter and chattering. Just say, 'Excuse me,' if you have to walk between two people yakking—so at least they won't think you're totally a comatosed vegetable with the personality of a *fern*," I rehearsed.

I walked home alone. Slowly. Why rush?

That night, after I was sure the banquet was well underway, I drove to the school with a neighbor friend who was in ninth grade. Wearing slacks and a sweater, I barely opened and peeked through the side door of the gym.

A fairyland! Roving lights! Glittering decorations from the ceiling. Small tables with candles, and Cinderalla gowns on fairy princesses on the arms of tuxedo-clad princes.

My face flushed; I felt the flood of tears in the back of my throat.

"Don't let anyone see you! They'll know you feel rejected! And face it! You *are* rejected! Have some pride! Leave!" I ordered myself.

"Let's go. I don't want anyone to see us," I whispered to my friend.

"Oh, no! I want to watch for awhile!" she wailed. "I can't wait until I'm old enough to go! I want to see more!"

"I'm going. I'm sorry," I said, as I looked around the corner.

Walking out to the parking lot, I grew nervous. Maybe I would run into friends and classmates who had just stepped out for a bit of fresh spring air—dreaded thought!

I looked about the lot before leaving the building. All was clear. I ran to the family station wagon, pulling my neighbor by the arm. Driving home, I hunched over the wheel.

"What's wrong? You look so sad," my dad said, as I walked into the house.

"Oh, nothing, Mom and Dad," I said, going straight to my bedroom.

But, my dad followed me. I sat on the pillows and he sat on the end of the bed.

"Dad, don't you think every girl should get to be dressed in a formal gown accompanied by a guy in a tuxedo for her senior year? What kind of future do I have? I can't face the other kids! They *know* no one asked me—not even a *clod* with bad breath. I'm rejected. Dad, what's wrong with me? Am I ugly? I know I could lose ten pounds...." I cried while Dad listened.

I described the good fortune and beauty of the other girls for an hour, until I was saying the same things over and over again.

While wiping the tears from my face with his big hands, Dad said one thing, "Just be true to the Lord, Honey."

He *didn't* pooh-pooh the senior banquet and say, "Good grief! In a year the whole silly affair won't mean a thing. It's not a big deal later in life. You'll laugh about it someday. Those kids probably aren't even having a good time."

Instead, he just said those simple words. They never left me. They are etched forever in my memory.

And do you know what? He never said them again. He was brilliant. He must have known once was enough.

The secret of singleness at its best is not having somebody love me, but my loving others.

The only thing that matters in life is what we do with Jesus Christ.

Understanding God's Love

My friend asked me, "Why doesn't your dad *do* something about your brother? He's such a rebel! He keeps getting kicked out of school for mouthing off to the teachers, and he even got into trouble for something stupid like vandalism. I mean, don't you resent the fact that your dad keeps forgiving him over and over? Look how he has humiliated your family in this town. He doesn't deserve your dad; but your dad keeps giving him love and even *admiration*. I've only heard your dad speak with praise for your brother—his accomplishments on the track team, his swimming, and painting the house! Why does he speak so highly of him? Is he blind? I can't understand it, Käaren!"

"Jaynee," I answered, "many times I have been angry, because I thought my dad should have thrown him out of the house and disowned him." [I couldn't face the kids at school or the people in our little church. Many days I claimed I was sick and didn't go to school.] "But," I told her, "when I saw my dad's love and forgiveness—and the way he still admired my brother—I got a glimpse of the infinite love, forgiveness and admiration God has for *you and me*. By seeing the way my dad reacted to my brother, I saw that NO MATTER WHAT . . . we are God's children. And nothing we ever do will take away His love for us. My brother proved that."

"And you know what else, Jaynee," I continued explaining to my seventeen-year-old best friend, "my dad did something else: one day I overheard him while he was talking on the phone: 'Yea, uh, Mr. Wingstrom . . . ah-h, this is Al Witte, your neighbor down the street. Listen. I know things look pretty bad right now. But I want to tell you . . . you have a good boy. And he's going to turn out just great. . . .' "

"Do you remember when Tom Wingstrom got caught drinking and got kicked off the track team, and when it was in

13

the paper about his Halloween pranks and vandalism on Main Street?" I asked Jaynee.

My dad kept loving my brother. He kept believing in him although my dad's heart, I'm sure, felt like it was being cut out. He kept "seeing" my brother . . . not as he was, but as he would become—a good citizen and a Christian. (And he did become just that.)

God takes our past, our failures and mistakes, and forgives so perfectly that when He looks at us . . . He sees Jesus.

August 1973

He Has A Plan

Jesus was saying in that still, small voice . . . "Käaren, I have an adventuresome, beautiful plan for your life. I'm going to bless your life and ministry *above and beyond anything* you could ever dream or hope for.

Oh, you might not like it in the beginning.
You'll think I don't love you.
You may not understand me.
You'll hurt, you'll cry, you'll call for help.
And I'm asking you to trust Me.
I'll always be there.
I'm going to ask you to go through
Sorrow,
Pain,
and some suffering.

But I have chosen you to show your world that I will carry you through the bleak, frozen winters of your life. The world will be sure nothing will ever grow again. But put your hand in Mine. Show the world you're a *victor, not a victim!*"

I answered; *"Jesus, there will be times when I won't be brave. I'll want to bail out. I'll tell you I don't care about any great ministry. But I know you'll be faithful to me. Even when I disappoint you."*

When the Obstacles Are Big, You've Got to Dream Bigger!

"Look, I'm 26 years old. The only thing I want to do is to get married and have a family," I told my pastor-counselor.

I had stored in my hope chest everything from linens to spices. I was just waiting for the day to marry.

So far, the day had not come.

I cried the most at weddings. (And it wasn't just the tender ceremonies.) I could become an emotional basket case just walking through Dayton's department store watching the brides-to-be select their silver and china patterns.

"Käaren," the counselor pleaded, "you must believe that God can give you an adventuresome opportunity other than marriage. You must focus on Jesus Christ and *His* purpose for your life. Once you find that, you will be fulfilled."

"I told you! The only thing I want to do is get married and feather a nest. Can't you understand? There are laws written on the heart of a woman by God himself," I cried, pounding my fists on the arms of my chair.

"Isn't there anything you're interested in? What did you major in?" he questioned.

"Look! I'm from a small town in Minnesota. I taught high school for one year and before that I had the illustrious career of waitressing at Al's Friendly Diner." I challenged. "I did major in Communications, but I know I would never get a break in that field."

"Käaren," he pressed, "please take this piece of paper and write down one goal."

I stared at the paper for a minute. I didn't move. Finally I wrote:

Dear God,
    I give up.

            Love,
            Käaren

He read the note. We joined hands across the desk and I repeated his prayer after him:

"Dear God, I accept your Plan for my life. I trust you completely and believe that you only have my best interests in mind. I will believe that whatever you do, you do in love—even when I don't understand you. I believe you are the God of miracles, so today and always I will dream! And please cause your Holy Spirit to remind me of my focus, Jesus Christ himself."

"Now, dream big!" He challenged, after the hearty amen.

Three weeks later I was still praying. The emotional hold which had been paralyzing my creativity was lifting.

One ordinary afternoon, I decided television needed help—my help.

"*I* could think of better TV programs than this!" I grouched to a friend as I changed the channels in disgust.

"Go ahead! Call up the stations. Tell them what great ideas you have for new TV programs! Do it now!" she challenged.

I opened the yellow pages to TV stations and began dialing. I left the biggest station for last—WCCO-TV. And it turned out that it was the *only* station interested in hearing about my great, fresh ideas.

I made an appointment and put down the phone. I stood dazed and prayed: "Dear God! What *are* my great ideas, anyway?"

I knew one thing. I walked with the Creator of this universe, and He had a very good track record for creativity: planets, galaxies—the whole universe—and billions of people all so dramatically different. Plus, He said that I could be all that He is just for the asking!

The Lord dropped ideas into my head. I'm sure of it.

Two weeks later, I was sitting in the program director's office with an idea: a format called "Years to Youth" which had inquisitive junior-high-schoolers interviewing fascinating old people in their 80's and 90's (an inventor, a big-game hunter, a song-and-dance man from Vaudeville, an actress, etc.). WCCO-TV loved the idea, and they allowed me to write, create and co-produce the prime-time series, which we worked on for one year. (They also gave me a new car and an expense account!)

I'll tell you about the kind of experience and background which gave me the confidence to go into the number-ten-rated TV station in the country and actually believe *I* could help them out with their mediocre TV program . . . when they had stables of creative, expensive people at their disposal!

Are you ready? My experience included one year of teaching high school in a small town, and, of course, the four years of waitressing at Al's Friendly Diner!

See? I don't merely believe in miracles. I depend on them!

But God wasn't going to stop dreaming and planning for me here. More TV would follow, radio series, and books.

God was waiting for me to give up—not on Him, but on myself.

Temptation

Bob was a Christian film maker. I was fascinated by him! I enjoyed watching him and listening to him.

When the ladies sat in the kitchen at a party, I was sitting with Bob and the other men—because I was interested in their work. They were flattered. I probed, and picked their brains and imaginations.

"Wow! What ideas! Sheer genius! I admire you!" I'd react, as they spoke.

Secretly, I felt proud that I wasn't like the other women sitting in the kitchen talking about labor pains, Pampers, and the PTA.

And I hoped the women noticed that I was a woman who could dialogue with the men. So what if I didn't have a husband! I loved this circle of masterminds and power. For once, I belonged too!

I was getting high on this new sensation and attention.

"Now don't get giggly and silly or you'll blow it!" I scolded myself. "If they think you're an empty-headed female, you'll be in the kitchen!"

Bob had flashing eyes and dimples you could fall into. I rejoiced at every fun moment in his company.

Bob—a smooth man, warm and charming, friendly. Easy, relaxed, laughter that surfaced easily.

And *then*—I heard that Bob was separating from his wife!

"Jesus, I am struggling," I cried. "You know my heart, my thoughts. Cleanse me! Hear my cries! Save me from my thoughts and myself. I confess these thoughts to you. In Jesus' Name." And I didn't sit in Bob's circles anymore.

There Is Always Hope

"I can't stand her! I just can't tolerate her," Allison lashed out as we began talking after a meeting where I had spoken. "This lady at my church is such an insensitive jerk! She makes me furious."

"Why do you say that?" I questioned. Moments before, Allison seemed to be a warm, laughing young woman.

"Oh, she keeps saying things like, 'Not *everyone* can get married, you know, Allison.' She keeps telling me how God has *called* me to be single! Aren't *I* the one who decides whether or not God has called me to be single?" she continued, raging and waving her arms.

Allison was 5'8", thirtyish and weighed in at about 190 pounds. It's tough—living in a media-controlled society where only the size-eight woman gets lauded, paraded, and pampered.

Allison felt society's pressures from being thirty and single, I'm sure. And she didn't need somebody else killing all hope for her!

"Allison, I will believe with you. I will claim that God will give you the desires of your heart," I said, reaching up to her fleshy shoulders with both of my hands.

"Jesus," I began to pray in that parking lot, "Allison has a longing in her heart for a husband, children, and a home. I pray, that until the time comes in your plan to answer that prayer, you will fill her life with opportunities—ones that will glorify you before this society and world. You've always drawn people by your miracles. I know you will continue to do so. And we're asking you for one of those miracles. Or maybe two or three—right now."

"But, the lady in my church keeps telling me about *statistics*," she fumed, " '*Statistically* not every woman can get married.' But I don't give two hoots about statistics!" she announced.

"Our God is still a God of miracles today, that defies statistics," I offered softly. (I was disappointed that she hadn't changed her attitude toward the woman after my praying and counseling!)

"Jesus! Change this heart!" I telegraphed heavenward while she talked.

Then Allison mellowed. She wrapped her huge arms around me and said, "Thank you. You've given me hope. And without hope, I just couldn't go on."

As Allison walked across the parking lot, she held her head high, with a new air of confidence.

I hoped she wouldn't turn around, because she may have thought I was just gazing at her huge frame. But I was praying, "God! Again I ask you to work a miracle in her life!"

Hope. There's something about it. People will love you for it when you show them how to bask in it. Stripped of hope, they are devastated.

And it's a funny thing—it only takes a few minutes to inject hope. You can watch it go pumping right to the heart, and change the whole outlook.

March 1977

Looking Back

I wanted to write a book so I could dedicate it to my dad. I wanted to say: "Because of his love, I can just begin to understand the love of God."

How did it happen? I often wondered. Dad came from a broken home in the back hills of North Dakota during the Depression. He didn't have a father while growing up. But he knew how to be one. I found out.

Although I grew up shy, and socially slow, I still knew I had one great pal—my dad. We hugged, kissed, clowned around and joked until I was 15 or 16.

"Oh! You two! Käaren, settle down!" Mom would say, when I got carried away with Dad rolling in gales of uncontrollable laughter.

"She's okay!" Dad would call back to Mom, "one day she will have outgrown me!"

"Never!" I'd cried back, wondering why he would ever think that.

But, the time came. I did grow up. But memories remain.

Dad taught me to ride a bike, swim, dive, count calories, do higher math, write essays, give speeches, and drive a car.

He was clever, too. How does a dad get his young daughter to use the seat belt even if it wrinkles her new dress? He only had to say it once (that was all that was necessary): "Remember, Honey, you're not going to get any better-lookin' flying through that windshield!"

It's been said that the greatest thing a father could do for his children is love their mother.

Dad never needed "buddies," or the "boys," bowling, poker or much golf. Being with Mom was his favorite pastime.

With a lapful of boxes and bags, he would sit patiently in the women's clothing department scrutinizing the new outfits Mom was trying on.

"Let's see the flip side," he'd smile, as she did a three-quarter turn as though she were in the Miss America Pageant.

(Later this same year, Mom died in his arms after a month-long battle with cancer. At her last breath he whispered, "I will always love you. Forever. I'll be with you soon. I now put you into the arms of God.")

My dad—he gives me a glimmer of the unfathomable love of God.

June 1977

The Sunday Watch

I wonder....

Do the couples and the families at my church know I watch
them?

I *study* them.

I notice how they treat each other.

Sometimes, I rejoice—I see how beautifully God has
matched them.

Sometimes, I'm glad I'm single.

Sometimes, I am envious, and struggle to rid my heart of
that sin which could eat away my peace.

Do they ever think about me?

I wonder....

Do they ever ask what I do after church on a Sunday afternoon?

They probably think since we have a singles' group, my time
must be packed with fellowship!

They see me as Miss Friendly, Outgoing.

They even tell me so.

But do they ever stop to wonder if I need to have one special
person in my life, too?

Sometimes, I hope they don't.

But that's my pride. "Don't blow the Susie Sunshine Image,"
I tell myself.

They see me sitting in the front row of church singing my
heart out—with a mediocre voice at that.

I honestly try to keep my eyes on that altar and cross when
the envy and self-pity stab at my heart.

Otherwise, I would see couples sitting close, holding hands,
and smiling at each other.... And nudging each other with
their elbows at the Pastor's quips.

They must have secrets.

Special, private thoughts between the two of them.

I watch their children, and think of them as products of their love.

They would be surprised, if they knew what I was thinking.

But they should know that everyone—no matter how cheery—has a personal cross. And when the hurt hits a nerve, that one can cry a river.

Do you know what?

Sometimes, I'm afraid to say I hurt.

Will these people laugh at their couples' socials and say I'm just another pathetic single girl who's just man-crazed?

But, maybe, if I start letting people look inside my heart, they would let me do the same with them.

I wonder. . . .

What would happen if we all took down the walls?

August 1977

Saying Goodbye

After what was to be a simple gall-bladder operation for my mom, I called the doctor.

"Uh—I can't really tell you on the phone. I want to talk to you in person." The doctor spoke reverently.

"What. . . ." I hesitated. I knew something was wrong. "Just tell me! Is she alive?" I screamed.

"Oh yes . . . but there are complications."

"What complications? I need to know. I'm three hours away from the hospital. Is it cancer? It *is* cancer, isn't it— *tell* me!" I implored.

"Yes . . . I will tell you then, it is cancer. We are 99% sure. The liver is badly damaged. I want to express my deepest sympathy to you," he spoke in a rote, programmed way.

The next morning I was at Mom's bedside. Now God had to heal. He just had to!

"God! You hold the power! You've got to heal her. She's young. I'm younger. I'm single. I need her. You can't take her . . . not until I'm married," I pleaded.

But later that night, when I had left Mom in the intensive care unit, I was sitting in the absolute stillness of my bedroom. "Lord," I whispered, "if this cancer will bring a greater love for *you* in me, then I should say, 'Go ahead, take her.' But I can't. You've got to do the impossible—change me. You used the suffering of your own Son to bring about the healing of the world— so in this crisis, help me to bear a testimony of that grace. Help me believe that *whatever you do, you do in love . . . even when I don't understand You!* Because, right now, I *don't* understand you."

I continued to stare into the night. Dawn came. God allowed the world to continue on for another day—and I wondered why.

"Lord!" I called out, "your reputation is at stake. You *need* this miracle in this town. These people think this newly born-again doctor of ours has gone off the deep end. If you use this to show them the power of healing . . . YOU WILL PROVE YOURSELF! You'll have more credibility in this town!"

After a week of praying, I wanted to quit.

"This is a trick of Satan," I thought, "he wants me to hate God. This is a spiritual battle. I'm not going to give up."

I kept repeating the verse: "By His wounds we are healed." (1 Peter 2:24, NAS) I claimed that promise—no matter how black things looked.

With this confidence, I went back to Mom's bedside. I lifted up the blankets. No change. Her legs and feet were still huge and swollen.

I flopped my head on her chest. I was giving up. Again. And she knew it.

She dropped her arm with a thud on my back and whispered: "Honey, we've got to be strong."

Alone, once again I cried to God, "I'm single. You know that. I have no other family. Parents usually die when they're in their seventies or eighties. She can't die now! Don't you see? She will never see me as a married woman . . . or see my children."

God spoke over and over in my mind: *"I want to take your mother—my very own ransomed child to be with me. I've been waiting for her. She will be loved forever. Will you let me take her now?"*

God's faithful Spirit was praying for me to release my mother.

"Jesus," I prayed, "You came to save our souls and renew our spirits. Everything else is secondary."

Death has always seemed so far away. Now I was looking into its face. I wasn't prepared for this part of life. Nor did I want to be.

Sometimes, when the drugs wore off a bit, Mom would say

things like, "Always remember, Honey, when you made me happy and when you broke my heart, I still loved you. I always forgave you."

It's a funny thing. Only a parent can do that—and Jesus.

Four weeks had passed. Mom's eyes were circled with a blue-black color.

I reached for the guitar and we sang hymns, but afterward I held Mom, as I knew we were ushering her into eternity.

"Lord Jesus," I began, "this is my mother. Nobody can take her place. Although you have chosen *not* to heal her, I will believe that all things—even Mom's dying—will work together for good for us because we love God. Jesus, I now release Mom to you. I know you want her. In the Name of Jesus Christ, who tasted death for all of us, I pray. Amen."

As I sat watching her breathe heavily in the sanctuary of that room, I felt a quiet splendor. God's Spirit had triumphed.

I went to the kitchen for coffee. Dad continued the vigil. When I came back, he whispered while standing and letting the tears fall on the bed, "She's gone, Honey. She is with her Saviour now. Forever."

Dad held me and said, "Don't cry, Honey. She's with the Lord now."

We had been two hearts pulling the same load. Now the journey was over.

Later that day, I walked outside. The sun was shining. "Why? Why is the sun shining?" I wondered. The wind blew strands of hair across my face. I looked up into the face of God, and whispered, "Lord Jesus, you just use death to take us from one realm to another. Tell Mom I miss her. But, I am rejoicing— for one of us is with you.

The testimony of the dying will win the world to Christ.

God doesn't say, Don't cry. Don't grieve. Don't hurt. He only says, Don't fear.

September 1977

A Letter From Mom

My Dear Käaren,

Honey, if I must leave this world, I accept it as God's will, but right now I want to tell you so much.

I know you are trusting God for a wonderful husband. I know you have prayed since you were a teenager. And you struggle with the wait.

It seems like just yesterday when I first got a glimpse of you . . . as my baby girl! I savored the events of your life in my mind the first time I held you. What glorious things would be mine to share with you! I visualized your first steps, your first prayer, your first day of school, your high school events—starring in the school plays and winning on the debate team! I "saw" your college graduation day—and your wedding day. (I wore powder blue, of course!)

I don't know why God has delayed marriage for you. But, Honey, you must believe that you are a lovely, feminine young woman, and both your dad and I have said that you would make a dream wife.

I have never given you a marriage book. I felt Dad and I were the best thing you could read.

But before I leave you, I want to give you my thoughts so you will have them forever.

Never stop believing that God has "His man" for you. The pieces will fit together. You will not have a relationship that is like trying to make round pegs fit into square holes. You won't have the uneasiness that you have had in other relationships. When God gives you His special gift, my Darling, there will be a perfect peace. You'll recognize it. You'll rejoice in it! And your personalities will blend. When you meet, you will think that you've known each other your whole life. You'll pray, talk, and laugh together so naturally, and you'll see God is moving you both in the same direction in life.

29

So, please wait for that special man that God has for you. He will love and follow Christ like few men you have ever known—I'm sure of it.

Claim it! Don't listen to Satan's lies. God wants Christian marriages—for they live out the drama of the saved in union with Christ! It's what God dreams for you! Now take authority over Satan and his lies—in Jesus' name. For the enemy can't fill your mind with lies, nor can he block the relationship.

I can now leave you in peace, praising God, for I am leaving a daughter whom I know will never settle for second best—no matter how long the wait.

I've been proud of the love you have had for your dad, Honey. You admired, revered, and respected him. Honey, you should know how much joy this brought to his life!

Life got tough out there for us—when we lost money, and two businesses . . . but your dad said while crying in bed one night, "No matter what—I'm saved by Jesus Christ, and I have a wife and kids that love me like a father could only dream about. That part of my life is almost too good to be true."

I know you will transfer this same appreciation, gratefulness, admiration, support, and respect on to your husband. I know you will make your children see him as their hero.

Honey, your precious husband will be able to take all the madness the world has to give if he knows he's got a sweetheart waiting for him *at his address.*

So think of it as serving *Jesus Christ himself . . .* when you iron his clothes, make the meals, and clean the bathroom sink.

But, remember, there may be differences at times between you. He will be tired, discouraged, and upset at times. Sometimes, he will be so lost in thought he won't listen to your detailed account of the day. He may be working on papers inside his briefcase, but don't mistake this for neglect. And when you slip into bed together at night, don't pull away from him because he forgot to cultivate enough romance that day.

He's only a human being.

As you do now, single and alone, so then, ask Jesus to meet your needs and longings. (And I know He has done that for you continually as a single young woman.)

Remember the importance of always staying beautiful, fresh, and sweet in spirit . . . and appearance.

You will find joy when you sacrifice to serve one another. The world's philosophy today says it's every man for himself, but that's not God's way to happiness.

The real test of your love will be in your willingness to sacrifice! To get up and answer the phone when *you're* tired. To sweetly change plans when a looked-forward-to-weekend must be canceled. To wait without complaining when the new furniture or redoing of the bathroom gets postponed until business improves or the raise comes through.

I know it won't be easy to give in to the other's preferences, but you will have a power which the women's movement knows nothing about.

Your strength and power will come instantly with the calling of one Name . . . silently or softly . . . "Jesus." He heals, erases, soothes, and forgives. Instantly. That name will stop rebellion, pride, or a sarcastic remark.

And, Honey, when your husband comes home and announces he's lost his job or you're being moved, or your child is sick . . . just remember how to spell hope: J-E-S-U-S.

As I come to the end of my life's journey, I look back in wonder. God carried us through every sorrow and problem just like He promised He would. My only regret is that I didn't just trust Him at the *beginning* of every conflict, crisis, or hurt.

Give! Sacrifice! Serve! And *love*! With all your heart. And if you do, you are in for one of the richest rewards in life—a God-designed marriage.

I love you, my darling, laughing young woman. And I know I would have loved the precious husband God has for you. God will bring you both together in His perfect timing. Since I first held you in my arms, I've prayed for your husband—an unknown face and personality—yet a real person and a promise.

So give him my love and tell him I have loved him through prayer and believing.

Honey, embark on the greatest adventure with the joy of anticipation!

I'll meet you in the morning. We'll rejoice. And we'll understand it all in the bye and bye—beyond the sunset.

> *My love forever,*
> *Mom*

November 1977

Thanksgiving Day

Lord Jesus, you thought I was special. Didn't you?

You have this calling on my life . . . and have asked me to stay single.

You know there are worlds to conquer and minds to reach before I can be called to slice cucumbers in a food processor.

I feel alone today—Thanksgiving, 1977.

The first one without Mom.

Am I participating in your suffering, Jesus?

You have promised to reward and bless me for it.

But on this Thanksgiving Day, without a home full of family and turkey, it's hard for me to be what you called me to be.

You could have chosen other single women.

Those who are braver, stronger, less emotional, and dependent.

You're still in the business of performing miracles today.

And I need one in this heart of mine.

Give me the *victory*—because of Jesus. But, to begin with, let me praise you. . . .

Temporary Relief

A young woman sobbed on my living room couch, "I am so empty... *I want to get married!* So what, if it isn't God's first choice for my life! Second or third best would surely be a lot better than *this* miserable existence."

Three months later she met a young man, and within three months they were married. She did it! But, four months to the date of the wedding she was back crying on my couch.

"I feel so lonely again. Whenever my husband is gone, I feel so lost and empty—even sometimes when he's there! I guess what I really needed was *more than a husband.* But I don't know what."

"It's a strange thing," I began. "Another person might give temporary relief from the devastation of loneliness, but we all need to have inner strength and security of our own. Each person must be complete in himself. When we are whole, functioning people we discover our *own happiness.* This gives us individual meaning and purpose in our *own life,*" I tried to encourage her.

Of course, I had said this many times before to her. But now, after only a few months of married life, the painful truth rang out—loud and clear.

"I remember a young man I dated seriously," I continued. "His need to get married was overwhelming. It consumed most of his conversation as he talked about the agony of single life. That scared me! I certainly didn't want to marry someone so 'needy.' I wanted to marry someone who was alive, vibrant, 'high' on life, and involved in worthwhile, exciting plans, goals, and dreams!"

"But... I'm still so unhappy," she confessed, interrupting me.

"So much unhappiness results when we try to meet our needs through other human beings. And when people fail to meet our needs we experience unhappiness, loneliness, and frustration," I answered.

After I listened to a full account of her lonely evenings and the "hunting-widow's week-end," we prayed.

"Jesus . . . help us. Myself included. Help us to create our own life and ministry. The one you dream for us. If we are bored, we'll know it's because we don't have a dream. And God, we don't want to forget that we really do need each other. We need the encouragement, friendship, prayer, and love from others. But only you can give us fulfillment and meet the deepest yearnings of our hearts. YOU are the true source of contentment. Continue to remind us that we have the authority to say: 'In the name of Jesus Christ! I speak to my mountain: Mountain, be gone!' I believe you for a great dream for our lives! Amen."

Temptation Again

"Käaren, remember . . . even if you get laid off, I am still going to give you a big kiss goodbye at the end of the year!" One of my principals joked.

Since March, he had reminded me.

And I wanted him to.

He was a 6'2" giant of a man. Strong. Handsome. Authoritative. I admired his courage in controlling students and being a leader on the faculty. I respected him and would have done handsprings down the street to please him.

On my first day of teaching I slipped into his office and barely above a whisper announced, "Sir . . . you are a-h-h . . . my a-a-authority. I want you to know I recognize your position. If there is anything you must tell me or anything you feel you must reprimand me for . . . please do. I-I-I . . . know it will be to make me a better teacher. I won't resent it."

(I was nervous. I was hesitant in my speech, and forgot how to conjugate my verbs, so I knew when to quit.)

Anyway, he was uncomfortable. He nodded and nonverbally said, "I get it, Witte. Leave." Then verbally, he said without looking up from his desk, "Okay. Okay, Miss Witte."

I knew he was impressed. He didn't fool me by his aloof, "tough boss" act! And when my words had a chance to settle, he would realize the incredible thing I had just said.

In the following weeks, he tested my commitment to his authority—to the fullest.

"Ah, Miss Witte! Did you realize that three of your students were in the hall without a pass?" he questioned, crossing his arms, pursing his lips, and looking down into my flushing face.

"Oh . . . no, no I didn't. But, I will take care of it right away, sir."

And I was crying and screaming on the inside. He should

have known my brave-soldier bit was only an act in the name of professionalism.

Another time, he came pounding on my classroom door.... "Miss Witte! Did you realize that your students were throwing textbooks out the windows during your second-hour class ... at the custodian trying to mow the lawn!"

He paused and added, "They never did hit him."

What exquisite, comic timing he delivered on that unusual report! I felt the laugh almost surface! But I quickly gasped, and blurted out (straight-faced), "Ah, thank you, sir. I'll take care of it right away."

I didn't defend myself. I could have told him I didn't even have a second-hour class in that room. But I didn't.

"What's the use," I thought. "He was furious. He had to vent it on someone. Plus, I think secretly he knows I understand him. I see the grueling job he has—rebellious students, bomb threats, fires, screaming parents, vengeful, irate teachers."

I found myself putting little notes at the end of my office memos to him, like, "Thanks for being you! You encourage me! I appreciate you! I admire you."

I was beginning to develop "feelings" for him, feelings I had no business to feel. But he was a man I admired. And it was happening.

Halfway through the year, the tide turned. Smooth sailing. He began giving me warm pats on the back and compliments like, "Miss Witte, you're so easy to get along with! You're a doll! Listen, I've never said this before, but you are the sweetest, most delightful teacher I've had on my faculty in twenty years!"

Sometimes he would take my hand and hold it while he talked.

I was facing temptation. God was whispering my name. I knew why.

"Dear God, help me to see where this could lead— broken lives, children hurt. Oh, it looks so warm and innocent right now. Jesus, help me to realize that it is

37

serious. *Help me not to be flirty, cozy and overly charming... I have been. I confess it. It was all so subtle. Rescue me. Now! I choose to refuse these thoughts and turn my back against my wrong feelings,"* I cried alone in my classroom.

After composing myself, I wiped my eyes, and slipped the perfume spray-bottle back into the desk drawer without using it this time, before heading to the office.

We remained good friends. He confided in me about his tough job. He still patted me on the back occasionally. But I took it differently. And I still told him once in a while that I admired him, but my motives were pure.

I was free.

On the last day of school, before saying goodbye to him, I sat in my empty classroom. It was quiet and warm from the June sun. The bookshelves were empty, with all materials in storage. I thought back to my victory.

It was a victory that had needed to be reclaimed a few times, however. When I would have wrong thoughts, I'd grab myself and say, "Listen, Käaren! That struggle was settled. It's dead. Refuse these thoughts!"

The victory held to the last day, and would prepare me for future situations. I was learning how to live with unfulfilled desires. Resisting temptation, getting the victory—a transferable skill that teaches us about making choices—to sin or not to sin.

The school building was quiet. The kids had gone. I was the last teacher to check out. I slipped into the principals' office.

"I want to say goodbye now," I smiled, "it's been a great year. I admire you and want to thank you for being my friend. You taught me a lot."

He inched around the desk with his big frame and lightly put his arm around me and laughed, "You're a real doll. Listen, if there's anything I can ever do for you, let me know."

We exchanged more light conversation. I told him I would be doing some writing and hopefully another teaching job would open up. Then I left.

Walking through the parking lot, which was now empty except for my car, I cried, "He's so dear. His hug was so caring—but, I'm sure it meant nothing to him." I was struggling again.

"Dear God, I've got to be honest with you! Maybe I don't want these thoughts to die. I know I should have refused such ideas the instant they began growing in my head a year ago. I should have watched for them. But I didn't. Oh, God. I want to do what is right. Please don't let me see him. He must never know how I feel. Protect me! I will be strong. I am a new creature! I settle that again! Now!"

I prayed continually during the next week. I suspected he might call me. Of course, it would be something professional and casual: "Let's have lunch and discuss your teaching ideas so I can convey them to the new teacher next year."

It would be easy and innocent.

I praised Jesus it didn't happen. But I continually pray, "Jesus, help me to avoid anything stupid. You've given me a beautiful life. Help me to be aware of wrong thoughts—I am such a vulnerable woman. Help me never to disappoint you or hurt your reputation."

This was hard for me to write. But, dear reader, I wanted you to know. Maybe you'll have to make choices—choices that will tear up your insides. Choices that will cause you to cry out to God.

But there is a way of escape. I found it.

You Can Trust God (Ask Michelle)

"When it's the right time in your life, God will reveal that right guy for you. Wait, and prepare for that." I counseled a young woman after I spoke at a singles' conference.

"But I get so discouraged," she moaned. "There are so many beautiful girls, and so few men. Maybe I'll just marry a non-Christian, or a so-so Christian. I've had it with this trusting and waiting bit."

"Honey, God is preparing that man whom He will bring into your life. He is making that young man's eyes to see you as the most beautiful woman in the world. You will be the one he wants to spend the rest of his life with," I said, feeling the hurt.

"But, Käaren, don't you ever question God? Don't you ever wonder if He has forgotten you? I mean, don't *you* want to get married and have a family?" she demanded.

"Sometimes, I question God. I have a tough time trusting in that area of my life at times. Sometimes I manipulate God—I get others to pray hard for me, hoping that with the 'clout' of a group, He may realize how difficult my life is alone! But He loves me too much to listen to the wrong suggestions! I always end up asking His forgiveness for doubting Him. My life is in His hands. He is working out every detail. He has never failed me for one second of my life. He has a perfect track record. You can't argue with the facts!" I answered.

Elaine was a girl in her mid-twenties. No wonder she felt hopeless—this relentless society, with the barrage of Madison Avenue mentality and Hollywood ethics, could easily make a person feel like a worthless reject because she isn't a perfect size eight with clear skin and designer clothing.

(Elaine was at least fifty pounds overweight; she walked with a limp. She was wearing jeans with patch pockets on the back— not the Jordache look.)

I shared with Elaine an illustration God had given me a few days before:

I had been sent to various stores in another city to autograph books. I was introduced to the public relations man who would shuffle me around for the day.

"Hello, Käaren! I've heard so much about you! I've been looking forward to meeting you. And your book, *Angels in Faded Jeans* is fantastic. I laughed and cried reading it!" Ron pressed, shaking my hand warmly.

I couldn't believe the man who was speaking to me. What an incredible specimen of physical perfection! Looking up at his flashing blue eyes that spoke as much as he did, I guessed him to be about 26 and at least 6'2".

His crisp navy blazer and white shirt called attention to his bronzed skin and dazzling row of white teeth.

Throughout the day, I noticed heads turn. Indeed, he looked like a celebrity. But it was funny—he was unaware of the attention.

Early in the day, he shared his Christian witness with me. He then began telling me of the many blessings and miracles from God: "And two years ago, God gave me the most wonderful wife! What a precious gift!"

(Don't worry, I wasn't crushed! I had already seen the wedding band!)

I was fascinated by him! I watched his unguarded moments. I wondered, "What kinds of girls did he date before he was married? What kind of woman would a brilliant young man who went through school on scholarships and awards demand?"

I questioned and probed, especially regarding his relationship with his wife, Michelle—how they met, what attracted him to her, what was important to him, as a man.

I guessed her to be a born-again Farrah Fawcett-Bo Derek combination with the entire New Testament memorized, and for whom Proverbs 31 was personally written 5,000 years ago! Nothing less.

At the end of the autographing sessions, Ron asked me to join Michelle and him for dinner.

"Oh, no!" I groaned inside. "It's going to be 9:00 PM before we get out of here. I can't face going to a nice place for dinner, feeling like a greasy wreck, and then meeting his wife!" I struggled. "But I want to be gracious to this dear young man, I mean, after all those nice things he's said about me for two days—I must live up to them!"

We waited in the restaurant, and suddenly he stood up. I watched his handsome face glow even more than before as he evidently caught a glimpse of heaven. I knew this was the moment. The love of his life had arrived.

When she came to the table, I extended my hand, looked up and began saying, "I'm so happy to meet you. . . ." but I grabbed myself.

"Just act cool. Don't flinch. this is not her! In a split-second he will say, 'Oh, this is not my wife, this is . . .' just a friend or somebody. . . ."

That moment didn't come. In the next instant, he was graciously helping her with her chair. Tenderly, he placed a kiss on her cheek.

"Jesus, help me. Help me not to act uncomfortable. Help me to relax! She must have been hurt so much in life already. Please don't let my face betray my shock," I prayed silently.

Michelle's face was disfigured and scarred on one side, from what seemed to be severe burns. Her speech was even slightly affected.

Later in the evening, Michelle shared about her childhood accident with fire, and also how she had prayed for a husband. "God spared my life—He loves me. I wanted my life to glorify Him, so I accepted my condition, and God has blessed me. And look at the wonderful husband he has provided for me! I claimed that God would provide, and I never doubted it! I clung to the promises of Jesus, although I never had much affirmation outside those promises! But I didn't need man's affirmation! Jesus thought I was wonderful and precious! And I knew that

He was preparing the heart of some man to think the same about me. Then God gave me Ron. Don't you think he is the finest man God could possibly create?" she beamed, looking beautiful.

"Yes, Michelle," I agreed, giving her a gentle hug.

Then we all smiled, and rejoiced together at God's goodness.

"And, Käaren, I want you to feel free to share my story with other singles when you speak and write. Tell them that He is a faithful God."

That night, lying in bed, I looked up through my bedroom window at the stars and prayed, "Oh, God! I love you! Your power to move men's minds is far greater than the most high-pressured, intense, advertising campaign the media geniuses can devise! How faithful you are—even to a young woman like Michelle."

And yes, my dear Michelle, I am out there telling them. And I want you to know—you encourage hearts everywhere. You are precious. We love you. Thank you for loving and always believing in our God—*no matter what.*

God makes blind eyes see. And sometimes those that see . . . a little blind.

The Church Picnic

The picnic started at 1:00 PM on a glorious July day. I decided to arrive about 2:00.

Each family was to bring their own food. Games, volleyball, and a Christian singing group would follow. It was to be a "Jesus Festival," Minneapolis-style.

As the social director for the kids' games, I had looked forward to the event for two weeks. I planned games and bought prizes.

I also had one prayer for myself. "Lord, help some family to include me."

The day of the picnic, I wondered where I would sit with my little brown lunch bag. I knew and loved nearly everybody there. They were all my friends. Do I go to a table and ask to join them? No, surely somebody would wave me over to their table, when I walked from the parking lot to the picnic area. But then what *might* happen—suddenly, they would realize they should have included me! They would feel small and thoughtless! I couldn't face their embarrassment.

"Here, have some of our chicken and potato salad! We have plenty!" they might say, watching me take a cold meat sandwich out of my bag.

"Oh, Herb, we should have called Käaren! We drove right by her house!"

I just couldn't put anybody through that tension, I thought—"Skip lunch. Tell them you already ate."

Later in the afternoon, I spotted Ginny. "Hi, Ginny! When did you come?"

"Oh, I just got here." she said.

"Did you eat?" I questioned.

"Not here. I didn't have a family to sit with. Face it—as singles we have the constant problem—if we're not invited, we are alone! What do you do anyway—take your little lunch bag and sit on a blanket by yourself?"

"Oh, Ginny," I whispered, putting my arm around her, "if they only heard us talking! If they only felt what we are feeling right now! They would be so hurt. We just can't let them know!"

After the picnic, I drove home praying. . . .

"Jesus, forgive me for any self-pity. Thank you for helping me forget about myself by playing games with those bright, enthusiastic kids my friends have given us. Oh, God, if I am so blessed someday to have a family, help me to always look for the person that might need one. Thank you for giving me days like this because they will help me never to forget just how much a family including me today would have meant. And Lord, please help the families in our church to be sensitive to our needs, as singles, without it becoming a burden for them. I love them so much."

Soldiers in Old Lace and Velvet

"Käaren, please pray for me. I'm 30 years old now, and last night I lay in my bed and cried, while the tears ran into my ears. I've been faithful to God. I've obeyed Him. I've never slept with anyone. I've been a Sunday school teacher, led Pioneer girls, and sung in the choir. I've kept myself attractive. And I've trusted Him in this area of a . . . ah-h- . . . a mate, but I'm weary." Lynnette poured out her heart to me in the church foyer after a morning service.

I was surprised. Lynnette, a pretty businesswoman, seemed to ease through singleness with purpose, grace, dignity, and direction. Never in our eight-year friendship had she talked about tears and sobbing in the night.

I just listened, with my eyes burning into hers. My heart felt her ache.

I wanted to hug her and call out to Jesus with a simple, "Why, Jesus? I can't stand to see my sweet, delicate friend hurting so badly. It cuts me, too."

"Käaren . . . p-p-please pray for me. Please make that commitment, that you will pray for me. I just found out this morning that Diane got engaged. Käaren, why not *me?*" she pleaded, losing her composure.

"Let's sit over in the park across the street," I suggested. As we walked, I knew I could only tell her one thing. It wasn't the thing that she wanted to hear.

"Lynnette," I began, "we are followers of Jesus Christ. I can only pray for one thing in your life—God's glory—no matter how tough the assignment. I would not be doing you a favor if I didn't. Maybe God will choose to show His glory through a husband and a family. Maybe not."

"But, Käaren! I feel lonely and left out . . ." she wept, "I have

46

needs! And apparently you don't," she accused.

"I have needs," I whispered.

"I want a relationship and a loving home. I'm a homemaker, not a businesswoman, and I have never wanted to have a career. I wanted to have a husband and children. And he doesn't have to be the president of the United States, either. Just a simple, loving guy. Käaren, is it fair?" she continued.

It is always hard to pull somebody out of hurt. But when you personally know the hurt and ache they feel, it's extra hard. There is the temptation to question with them.

"Sometimes I feel like God is laughing at me . . . just dangling marriage over my head, letting me be alone and unfulfilled. Oh, Käaren, I know it's wrong. Jesus, forgive me. . . ." she confessed and prayed without taking a breath.

"Lynnette, you can be sure God's timing will be right. In His perfect time He will answer your heart's cry. He doesn't make mistakes," I said before praying: "Lord Jesus, I have asked 'Why' today. Lynnette has asked your forgiveness. I ask your forgiveness now, too. In your name, Jesus, we take authority over these negative thoughts. They are not from you. In the name of Jesus, I command that these wrong thoughts depart. We know where they come from, and they are not of God! Jesus, you died for such thoughts. We have the victory because of that. I know that you will give us the resources to live the way we should as singles for a productive, positive life glorifying to you."

"God . . ." Lynnette whispered, "I want the world to look at my life and say, 'because she lives a beautiful, wholesome life as a single, there must be a God. It's the only way it could be done.'"

"Lynnette," I said, lifting my head up and looking into her blue eyes, "we must continually remind ourselves that Jesus must be the total reason for our joy! We are saved! Rescued! Forever! Can you imagine? We walk with the Creator of this universe! The King of Kings! We must never lose sight of that wonder and fall into self-pity and questioning. Let's reconfirm ourselves right now together as soldiers, bondslaves to our great Lord and Saviour."

"Jesus, do whatever you will with our lives. We ask your forgiveness for making demands. We are yours. We have given ourselves to you, and today we renew that commitment. Our love, loyalty, and commitment to you will not depend on whether or not you give us a husband and a family." I prayed.

Lifting her face to the October sky, Lynnette added, "I am confident that you will meet the deepest needs of our hearts. You have always done it before. And I know you will heal these wounds, too."

We walked back to the church. It was empty. Lynnette went out the side door to the parking lot, and I slipped into the sanctuary.

I walked down the aisle without taking my eyes off the cross, but a thought pierced my mind: "Maybe the custodian or *even the pastor* will come through here." I knew they would think one thing, "There's another single girl on her knees begging God for you-know-what . . . ha, ha, ha. . . ." I could imagine them laughing their heads off with their families and friends around the sumptuous Sunday dinner table.

"Stop! Get out of here!" I commanded myself. "Don't let anyone know you come to the altar alone. They must think you have it all together, that you are balanced, strong, motivated, accomplished. You can't let down that image. You're a speaker, a writer. Leave! Now!"

But, with my eyes on the cross, my fear and pride dissolved long enough to bend down. On my knees, I slowly drew a cross with my finger on the carpet while saying, "Jesus, you died for these tears. I want to be a follower. I want the world to say *you exist* because of my life. So if I must pay a big price for that, I will. I bury my brokenness in the grave where you died. I claim my victory in your resurrection. And—I lift Lynnette up to you. I don't demand a husband for her. I only ask that her life bless the world—no matter what that takes. I love her too much to pray for *anything less*."

Walking back down the aisle, I saw the custodian come in to lock the doors.

I didn't look up.

He was a cheery, friendly family man, but at this moment he said nothing. He didn't even lock the doors after all. He just left.

I was grateful. I didn't need any chit-chat just then. Maybe he sensed that. Maybe he'd been a weary soldier once, too. Maybe he also had cried, "Why, God?" We all need at some time or other to renew our commitment to Christ.

Our purpose in life must be to give glory to God's Son and not merely seek happiness.

A Great Leap in My Single Bound

When it's January in Minnesota, and you're invited to do a television program for one day in Miami, you stretch that day to at least ten! Somehow.

On this trip, my friend Bernice was free to come with me. One afternoon as we walked along the coast feeling the sun warm our faces, we seemed to have come across a "couple's spot." The jagged, rocky coast and blue water welcomed the young—the lovers.

The couples—arms around each other, holding hands, gazing into each other's eyes—it was their way of responding to the glorious scenery.

So often before, I had longed to be with someone special, too. But, I'd come a long way, and I had a new idea: "Let's just sit and let our legs dangle on these huge rocks, face the ocean, feel the sun tan our faces, and sing praises to HIM!" I exclaimed.

We sang and harmonized songs from the Scriptures, and other hymns of praise. Like always, I needed to express what I was feeling! This was the ultimate! Praises to the great Creator!

Then sings my soul, my Saviour God to Thee. How great Thou art!

April 1979

Allan

"You probably don't remember me, but I was in the audience at a seminar you gave," came the voice on the other end of the line. "I just wanted to tell you it was great! You have a way of inspiring people!"

I remembered him. Believe me.

How does one forget a young man in the front row who looks as if he just posed for the cover of *Gentlemen's Quarterly?* Smiling. *Listening.* Laughing. Winking.

Now, on the phone, we made small talk about people we knew, discussed some books, and talked about his personal life.

Then he called again.

"I would really like to go out with you sometime. I would like to talk more with you," he said.

That was a hard moment—what could I say?

"Oh, a-h-h . . . how nice of you to ask me. I'm a bit pressed right now, perhaps you won't mind calling back tomorrow," I stammered.

Four years ago, I had decided that I would not date anyone unless the Lord clearly showed me it was to be a serious relationship. Someone who was going in the *same direction* in life. I knew that the Lord had filled my life with blessing and great privileges, and with that comes great responsibility. I had to date carefully—make good use of my time. I could not date indiscriminately so that the enemy could move in. I am vulnerable—and I know it. So does Satan.

For me, dating had always been time-consuming and unprofitable. And when a dating relationship ended, there was usually hurt and misunderstanding, and emotional problems to deal with for awhile afterwards. (Not to mention lost friendships.)

After talking with Allan, I asked for direction: "Jesus, is this what you want me to do? He said we'd discuss a prayer group he wants to start. But what about the next time? He seems so warm . . . and interested in me personally. . . ."

I got the answer. "Don't date him—even once."

But I wanted to go out with him. I wanted to listen to those compliments! "You're a great young lady! So attractive! I'm impressed! I want to hear more of what you've done!"

Allan was a young Christian businessman, but I knew the Lord did not intend this to be a serious relationship.

"Listen, I'm having a few people over for dinner on Thursday. Could you come?" I asked, the next time he called.

"Great!" he answered.

During the week, the others I had invited had to cancel. So Allan and I were alone.

After dinner we talked about growing up in a small town. And we laughed a lot. He listened to the boring details about my writing and other projects. He even encouraged me to talk!

"Käaren, I'm absolutely fascinated by you!" He laughed, patting my hand. "How about going to church with me tomorrow night? A local author is speaking."

I was silent. I felt the cold bite of having to make a decision. I was flattered and enjoying the attention.

"Say no! You know you're attracted to him! And he is to you! Say it! What can come of this? You know there are things in his past life that won't be right for you. Say it! Now!" I commanded myself.

"I really don't feel that I should date you, Allan. Please don't take it personally—but, I'm sure you understand, with my being in this ministry and all. Lots of travel. . . . But, I will join you this one time."

"Great!" he said, giving me the time he'd pick me up, as he walked out the door.

"God, maybe I do need to have my feminine ego touched up. Maybe I need to know that some man thinks I'm lovely and attractive. So, if I do need this kind of confirmation and attention, does that make me totally wrong?" I cried. "You have provided wonderful husbands for other Christian women. I have no one to tell me he thinks I'm lovely. You made me a woman, didn't you? This is a real need I have."

One month passed since that first dinner at my house, a month filled with concerts, dinners, tennis, and writing "comedy material" by the edge of the health-spa pool!

"Jesus, why don't I have peace about this relationship?" I struggled. "Why does your voice always say this is not your perfect plan for me? Why can't I have your blessing on this?" I cried and sobbed one day as I sat by the lake. "Okay. Okay. I give up. But you've got to perform a miracle in my heart. Please forgive me for the way I have talked to you. If I knew what you knew.... Please work in Allan's heart, too. He may be deeply hurt. God, bail me out of this! Even when I don't want out! This is a good, wholesome, fun relationship! But I know it isn't what you have in mind for me."

"Listen, Käaren, dear sweet, Käaren," Allan began at dinner that night, "you're an outstanding gal. I admire and respect you. But as far as our relationship goes... well, uh, it just seems we aren't going in quite the same direction in life. My past life is so different from yours. Listen, you should marry a minister, or an evangelist, or a missionary-type."

I didn't say anything aloud. Just, "Thank you, Jesus," silently.

"I still want to be your friend. And I will be interested in your work, and your dreams and goals. I admire you, Käaren," he continued.

"Maybe I don't care about being admired. I need to be loved! As a woman!" I cried inside my heart.

That night at the door, Allan prayed. I don't remember what he prayed. I just said goodbye and smiled.

"Jesus, I've grieved you through this relationship. Forgive me. I want to praise you right now. I know I could have been spared from all this emotional upheaval if I had listened to your voice in the beginning. You make your will perfectly clear. Please give me the supernatural grace to do what you tell me after this...." I prayed with my head on the door, as Allan drove away.

It was final. I had escaped—but not without pain.

But the Lord continued to speak to me, "Käaren, my dear child, I love you too much to allow you to marry anyone less than the *perfect match* I have for you. And I want you to know something: I love you. I think you're beautiful."

I know he said that. I heard Him.

My sheep hear My Voice and they know it. — Jesus

Susan's Bridal Shower

Susan is twenty-four.

I'm thirty-three.

Her bridal shower was lavish and elegant. She was radiant in a yellow dress, a contrast against her tanned skin and lovely black hair. I looked around the huge living room that seated about thirty.

There were three groups:

> The middle-aged family ladies,
> Susan's just-past-college-aged-friends,
> And me!

Two ladies said to me, "You're next!! Yours will be the next shower!" Giggle. Giggle.

I forced a smile. Here I was, the obvious *single* girl from church.

I called a friend on the phone afterward. "Why can't I have a wonderful fiancé like Susan's Bruce? Do you know, Elsie, there are no men my age that haven't been married or don't have mixed-up lives? Why do I have to be the one who smiles through the showers and the weddings, and listens to the banter, 'You're next!' "

"Käaren, you're special. That's why." Elsie said softly, in sharp contrast to my whining. "Why did God let my Jim die in that motorcycle accident, so I now sit and watch other people's kids singing in church until I could bawl and run out? I'll tell you why, because God thinks I'M SPECIAL."

Closing the conversation on the phone, I prayed, "Thank you, Jesus, for making me so special."

You are special to Him, too.

God's Way of Doing Things

"God, give them your patience and grace! I'm lost and I'm late!" I cried, driving down a country road to a speaking engagement.

"Why do I have to drive to these remote outposts anyhow? Why can't I go to civilized places with road signs!" I continued to gripe to God on that painfully early morning. "Nine AM isn't early for those women to have a brunch, because they live close together. But, I've had to drive for two hours! Didn't they think of me? Oh, well, there'll probably be only fifty sleepyheads anyway," I continued.

I finally thundered into a large barn-like building, looking for the coordinator. It was packed, and hot—near steamy. Ladies fanned themselves as they drank coffee. There must have been close to *three hundred* ladies in a hall that should have held 150. Everything was wrong at this point, as far as I was concerned.

I finally found the coordinator and sat down. Then the lady on my right informed me of the curlers I had forgotten to take out of the back of my hair!

The coordinator-mistress of ceremonies made periodic announcements—without a microphone. I wondered why, because surely no one was able to hear her.

Then it hit me. *There is no microphone!*

"I don't expect rural America to stage productions like Radio City Music Hall, but really, a simple microphone for 300 people seems so minimal," I griped to myself.

"I need a microphone." I whispered firmly to the coordinator. "I have a *soft voice.* And with the acoustics in here, and all these small children, no one will be able to hear me," I pleaded.

The coordinator insisted they would be able to hear me. Nothing could dampen her excitement and enthusiasm for this event. Not even me!

"I'm really looking forward to hearing you! I've always want-ed to meet you! I've heard you on the radio, and seen you on TV! I've heard so many people talk about you!" she beamed.

"Thank you," I said with my head bowed. "I'm going to slip into the washroom. I must do something with my hair."

Now her radiance and spirit dropped a few notches. She fi-nally sensed the truth. I wasn't excited about being there.

When I pushed open the washroom door, I caught a glimpse of a face I hardly recognized. Mine!

"Jesus, I have a right to feel this way! Look! Those ladies and their kids surely don't know that I have some needs. They just want me to stroke them, tell them they're great, and that you have great plans for them. Well, nothing's going right today. So why put me into this? Why didn't you call someone else to this ministry? I know, I'm a griper, a complainer, a discontented single. And they probably have sensed that by now," I cried, as I noticed I 'still had another curler in my hair.

"Oh, Jesus, forgive me. I have the privilege of sharing you with these people. Please, forgive me," I sobbed.

The M.C. introduced me moments later in a loving way. She told them in detail about me. Why didn't she just say what I deserved: "Käaren is supposed to be a sweet young woman, but today I find her to be a difficult, impossible griper."

Grace.

"Good morning, ladies and daughters!" I began. "Today is a special day. You see, in the few minutes I've been here I have tested God. I was complaining and allowing Satan to put all sorts of opposition into my heart. But I have asked Jesus to for-give me. And He has. Now, I want to share the greatest thing that every happened to me—just how I got to know this Christ who forgives me, and loves me *no matter what.*"

As I began to speak, I noticed one man in the audience. He was in the back. Nearly unnoticed. But one glimpse of his face and body language made me gulp mentally. He was the Pastor!

"He hates me," I concluded. "I haven't said more than twenty words, so what's the deal? I got all the curlers out. I publicly confessed my latest sin. Did he feel threatened? Should the ladies have asked this man-of-the-cloth to speak instead of an ex-small-town-schoolteacher?"

"Don't say it!" Something cautioned in my head, as I was about to talk about being "born again."

Instantly, I felt I was being cowardly. "Someone will be offended," the thought struck.

I pushed the words back. Then they came again. I wondered why the caution. This had never happened before.

I was ten minutes into my message, yelling, and straining my voice (no mike). It got stuffier in the hall, and the restless babies went into action.

"Lord! Please!! How rude!" I yelled heavenward.

At one point, I stopped and looked at a woman with a one-year-old. The child was crawling on the table, pulling off the cloth, and with alternating screams, throwing things. I looked at the mother with *pleading* eyes.

"Please!! Give me a break!! I can't even be heard. Can't you see there's no microphone?" I begged mentally.

Three other babies were crying periodically.

I wanted to stop talking and say, "I give up. This is hopeless. There's a minister here who's doing a slow burn at me and now four screaming babies. And no microphone."

I cut the message short.

A group of people lined up to shake hands and get autographs. At the end of the line was the young woman who had been sitting in front of me with her unruly baby.

"Your talk has changed my life. I have hope now. I can trust Jesus Christ, because I see what He has done for you. I know He will do the same for me, Käaren, my dear," she choked and walked away.

I was stunned. How could she have heard anything I was saying?

As the hall emptied, the coordinator walked over to me with open arms. As she hugged me, she said, "Oh, Käaren, Käaren. You gave the gospel! You clearly told these dear people how to be born again! You see, these people don't hear that here. In fact, our pastor said that if the speaker mentioned the term "born again" he was going to stop the meeting immediately! And that young woman with the fussing child in front of you! You were so gracious! And I'm sure you didn't know that she has cancer, and that her husband is divorcing her. . . ."

My Father Will Take Care of It

My thoughts went back to my college dorm days—a particular Friday night. The floor was hopping. Girls were running in and out of the showers. Blow-dryers were roaring. Most of the girls were going to some party or gathering. Simultaneously, I was trying to blow-dry my hair and iron a blouse on a suitcase, when a girl from India came into our room to borrow a book.

"Here it is! I can't talk! I'm rushing to get to the game on time!" I furiously ironed.

"Käaren, may I speak to you for just a minute?" she asked.

"Yes. . . ." I paused, and looked up.

"I feel so sorry for you American girls. You're so pressured to be at the right place at the right time. You're always trying to be where the guys are. You hurry continually, for fear you will miss a certain guy and he'll date someone else. This is a sad way to spend your life. And then I see that you and your friends become envious and jealous of one another when one has a date or gets engaged," she confronted me softly.

"Oh . . . uh, I suppose you're right, Rashida. But it's the American way of life. And if you're going to be in this country. . . ." I smiled.

"Oh, Käaren," she interrupted, "I am totally relaxed. I don't have to worry! I know in the right time my father will introduce me to someone. He will do all the arranging. And that person will be perfect for me. For you see, our families will approve and share our love; we will be of the same socio-economic background; our ages will be right for each other; and academically we'll be suited. And most important of all, our religion will be the same.

"It's too important an area of life to take into my own hands. And I'm lifted of the concern! I'm free to enjoy my studies and stay in America!" she rejoiced.

I never forgot the analogy.

Timing

What a faithful God you are!
You'd never cause me to lose my dignity.
Those are the tactics the non-believing world uses.
You'd never say, "Look, you're on your own. Catch somebody
yourself."
I don't have to hustle in
singles' places,
or panic,
or be flirty and defrauding,
or date indiscriminately.
I don't have to strip myself of self-respect by wearing alluring,
sensual clothing.
I've given you my life.
I can trust you to arrange every detail.
Your timing is perfect—
never a second too early,
nor a second too late.
Looking back . . .
When I was five years old, the neighbors moved.
They left me a shiny ten-speed bike!
If I had tried to ride the bike then, I could have killed
myself!
The gift was wonderful! But the timing was all wrong.

August 1979

Open My Eyes, Lord

In the three years that I've lived in this Minneapolis-Lake Harriet neighborhood, I've shared my faith in some way with each neighbor.

Except one.

She lived in a strange, eerie house. It didn't fit into the neighborhood with all the other nice homes resting on lush-green lawns. The lights were rarely on.

Actually, I never saw anyone in the house; I heard that an old lady lived there. So, I crossed her off my list—she was too "spooky" for me.

"Strange lady—lives in a dark, dank house. The lawn is rarely mowed, and the weeds flourish," I thought.

"There's a fire!" A frantic neighbor yelled as she pounded at my door one summer afternoon. "Help! And there goes the fire truck . . . he's going the wrong way! Please come!"

In the next instant, I was out in the street shouting at the firemen with her. Finally, they backed up, and pulled into *the strange neighbor's driveway!*"

"Dear God! Don't let anyone be hurt!" I called aloud, watching the smoke gush through a slightly opened window.

The firemen pressed into the house. About a minute later, the three came out slowly.

"She's dead," one announced to another, pulling a hose from the truck.

"You mean, the lady of the house died?" I questioned my other neighbor.

"She didn't have a chance," the lady cried.

"What do you mean?" I begged.

"She was blind."

"Oh, no—no," was all I could say.

I needed to be alone. I walked away—around the lake. Life was going on. The joggers were running and huffing. Young mothers pushed their strollers. Guilt and remorse engulfed me.

"Dear God, forgive me. She wasn't weird or odd—she was blind. That's all. And she was the only one in my little corner of the world whom I didn't tell about my faith in Jesus Christ."

I've asked for another chance with other people. But this time there would be no second chance.

August 1979

Satan and the Single Girl

Our mind is our battlefield. Some people have obsessions—alcohol, drugs, or sex. These are Satan's strongholds. And he will use anything to make us ineffective—even an obsession to be married.

Satan puts wrong, destructive thoughts into our minds. He will tell us to take matters into our hands, and not trust God for a mate. Or he'll tempt us to wear sexy clothing, flirt, and defraud men. He'll say, "You'll be left on the shelf, if you wait for the Lord! You'd better marry *someone*! So what, if he isn't a great Christian! Just look at those unclaimed blessings—those old maids who waited and trusted the Lord!"

The Scriptures warn us not to listen to these lies.

When we see happy families or couples, the enemy may put thoughts of self-pity, envy, jealousy, and despair into our minds. These thoughts may cause us to blame God, or manipulate Him, become depressed, and date indiscriminately.

We can become slaves—bound by negative thoughts and feelings.

One author has stated the reason for Satan's plan of attack on us: "Satan is angry. You'd feel the same way if you were in his shoes. He lost his one big chance when Jesus refused every one of his tempting offers, resisting him all the way to Calvary. Once the Lord accomplished His mission on the cross, Satan's doom was sealed. He hates Jesus for robbing him of his last chance for survival. Ever since, he has devoted himself to striking back at the Lord. *But how can he do that?* The Lord is beyond his reach! Yes, but there's another way he can hurt the Lord: *By damaging his children.* When a child of God is abused by the devil, it causes pain to our precious Saviour. And the only way Satan can get even with the Lord is to use his power and advantages to keep people from coming to Christ, and after that, to keep them from maturing once they are saved." *

St. Paul wrote to the Ephesians: "Last of all I want to remind you that your strength must come from the Lord's mighty power within you. Put on all of God's armor so that you will be able to stand safe against all strategies and tricks of Satan. For we are not fighting against people made of flesh and blood, but against persons without bodies—the evil rulers of the unseen world; and against huge numbers of wicked spirits in the spirit world" (Eph. 6:10-12, TLB).

Encouragingly, Paul continues to tell us *we can make it*. "But to do this, you will need the strong belt of truth and the breastplate of God's approval" (Eph. 6:14, TLB).

"So use every piece of God's armor to resist the enemy whenever he attacks, and when it's all over YOU WILL BE STANDING UP!" (Eph. 6:13, TLB).

I am convinced. I've seen it in my own life and in the lives of others. Satan focuses on our singleness to sap our joy—to kill our desire to win the world for Christ, or even share coffee and our testimony with a neighbor. Being married can become more important than serving Christ.

God is asking us to use our years as singles to be *big producers*! He wants us to get direction for *His great plan for our lives*.

It's just like Satan to turn our times alone into a feeding ground for destructive obsessions. But God wants us to use these times alone to GROW IN HIM—a preparation time for the great plan He wants us to carry out for the rest of our lives! These are to be creative, building years! Not years of gnashing, anguish, and torment.

I wonder how many potentially great marriages, like those of Hudson and Marie Taylor, John and Betty Stam, and Jim and Elisabeth Elliot have been missed because the enemy has

---

*Quoted from *Help Lord, the Devil Wants Me Fat*, by C. S. Lovett. Used by permission.

65

pushed people into hasty, thoughtless marriages.

In wrong marriages, lives are destroyed, homes broken, dreams shattered. But Satan is subtle. He can make it look so right and justifiable. I know.

Marriage can become our God. And the first commandment says we must not have any other gods before Him!

Of course, Satan would have us believe that what he suggests are actually our own justifiable thoughts! He makes us think the ideas are good, right, and deserved! He disguises himself perfectly.

However, we can be the winners! Because we have authority—in Jesus' Name—over all the powers of darkness.

We can pray:

"Jesus, in the quietness of this room, please reveal the thoughts that block my fellowship with you. As you bring them to mind, I ask your forgiveness. God, fill me with your creativity, your power, your originality, your love . . . and lead me on to the great dream you have for my life."

September 1979

Burying My Rock Pile

"How dare that pastor be in the pulpit, much less on the radio! He can't even bring up his family right! Every time he starts talking about morals for young people . . . I cringe. After all, his daughter had a child out of wedlock, and his son was in jail for a year," I often thought as I heard him on the radio.

Occasionally, I alerted others to these facts.

"Do you think a man like this should continue in the ministry? I mean, don't the Scriptures teach that if a man can't control his own family, he is is no position to lead others?" I said to a friend. She agreed.

Then another friend reminded me: "Remember, he that is without sin, may cast the first stone."

"He's a liberal," I insisted.

Shortly after my first book came out, I was listening to the radio. This same Pastor's program began. Just as I started to switch the dial, I heard, "Hey! I'm so excited about a new book by a lovely young woman, Käären Witte! Her book, *Angels in Faded Jeans*, which is based on her teaching experiences, is highly recommended for every mom, dad, and teacher! Kids, too! Young people will get a glimpse of what a Christian teacher is like. I'm so proud of her! Listen! You'll fall in love with her as you read this book. I sure did!"

A week later, I was visiting a church where I had spoken to the singles' group the night before. I looked at the bulletin board and quaked: There was the name of this radio pastor! He was filling in for the regular pastor, from halfway across the country! Coincidence?

I began to feel the guilt of never having confessed as sin my critical attitude—toward a man I'd never even met.

About halfway through the radio pastor's message, the coals began to heap.

"I want to share a story," he began, "from *Angels in Faded*

67

Jeans, written by a lovely young lady who is also a guest here today—Käaren Witte. I'm so proud of her."

That was enough. I fell on my face before the Lord.

"Dear God, have mercy on me," I cried, while trying to hold up as members of the congregation turned around to smile at me.

Now isn't it just like Jesus to cause another servant of His—the very one we have criticized—to give us love, recognition, and encouragment? That's the kind of Saviour we have.

Prayer on a Monday Morning

Jesus, you have a right to my life.
I have given my life to you.
And you have taken my commitment seriously.
You want me to make a statement through my life.
You're not going to make mistakes.
You won't waste time, and you understand what is *best for me.*

Forgive me for fearing you'll do me wrong!
For thinking your wisdom will fail.
Or you won't understand what I need.
Or you'll give me second best.
Or you'll make me miserable, because I sin and disappoint you.

Somebody once asked, "How do you take this singleness in your life with the loneliness ... and the sorrow you've had. Do you just take it as it comes ... one day at a time?"
"No," I affirmed. "I took it IN ADVANCE with a commitment to Jesus Christ. I crossed that bridge before I got there."
Jesus, you are the basis for my joy. Not any talent, success or another person.
Because, when the talent dries up, and the people disappoint me, and the success shifts—I won't be without joy.
I have you.
And you are not limited by my wildest of dreams!
　Amen.

October 1979

Trust

"Käaren, I suppose when it's God's perfect timing to give me a husband, He'll give me a real DUD—a loser," Chris, my 35-year-old never-been-married roommate sobbed.

"The guy will be such an inept clod," Chris wailed, "he will probably wear three different plaids and think designer jeans are Oshkosh B'gosh overalls. He won't be able to take three words and make a sentence. And then God will say, 'Take him or leave him. This is the best you get.'"

"Chris! You and I don't know the same God! I've put my life in the hands of a God who has promised to do *far above* and beyond anything we could ever dream or *hope for*! (Eph. 3:20) And that includes a wonderful mate. Nothing less!

"And, Chris, when I travel across the country, and see great marriages I ask those couples, 'Did God give you a mate *above and beyond* what you ever dreamed or hoped for?' The answer is always yes," I continued.

"But, Käaren, I know God has forgiven me for my past and sins; but, still, somehow, I don't think he's going to bless me with a wonderful mate. His grace and love just won't cover a mate too!" she cried.

"Chris, when you get to know God, you'll begin to believe that God's *only* style of operation in the lives of His children is *above and beyond* what they could ever dream or hope for," I exclaimed.

Tell me. What do you dream and hope for in a mate? Now, wait until you see what God does with His imagination, connections, and riches!

Romans 8:32 says that God gave us His only Son. So after that awesome gift, everything else is just small change. He said he would "freely" give us all things!

I can trust Him! You can trust Him!

October 1979

Reflecting

Two years ago, I was a nervous schoolteacher. My vision for God encompassed only the kids in my blackboard jungle.

My school closed due to enrollment decline. The faculty kept asking me, "What are you going to do?"

I said I didn't know. But I did know that God would provide. Somehow. Some way. Sometime. Some place.

As my school year ended, my first book *Angels in Faded Jeans* got published. Then I was speaking to hundreds of people and doing talk shows.

Me. Your average, non-descript small-town person. (I never made all A's. I never was a cheerleader, or a majorette, or homecoming queen. I could write another book about all that, too: "The Senior Prom, Cheerleading, and Other Forms of Adolescent Emotional Brutality.")

I don't deserve this ministry or the life God has given to me. I can't fathom it. Grace—God's style. (I think I'm proof of pushing Him to the limits of His grace and patience.)

Who would have guessed this would happen? But I *should* have! Jesus Christ promised a great plan and surprise—in those years when I struggled with my singleness. That promise goes for EVERYONE.

When I was a student in Europe in 1971, I knew I needed a great purpose. I didn't have a Big Dream. God's Spirit came to me and revealed how I lacked that MAGNIFICENT OBSESSION IN LIFE—JESUS CHRIST.

When I changed our relationship from a ho-hum and almost negative-image-of-God viewpoint, my world of adventure began to happen!

I remember getting on my knees in the old dorm room in Paris and praying, "Jesus Christ, I want to know you! My total purpose and fulfullment must be connected to YOU AND YOUR MINISTRY. Give me a big, gigantic "impossible" dream for my life.

And do you know what? He's doing it.

Free To Be Me

Pursue love. Not marriage!
A great goal.
It's "freeing!"
In pursuing love I'm free
      to encourage,
      support,
      and serve men.
I'm free from the thought:
      "Is he THE ONE???"
I don't have to get uptight and self-conscious.
How warm and fulfilling.
A man and a woman meeting each other's needs as members
    of the family of God.
Don't you love it?

Christmas 1979

"I can't spend Christmas alone! I don't even want to be with friends or another family! I just want to be with some of *my own family.* . . . I'll call the airlines and get a flight. I'm coming to Florida, no matter what!" I cried to my dad on the phone.

It was four days before Christmas. Dad was sick with the flu in Florida. I had only four days if I were to fly down, because I had to speak at a conference the day after Christmas, back in the Midwest.

"But, Honey, you're going to be speaking in Florida for two months this winter. We'll be together then. It just doesn't seem practical or like good stewardship to come now," Dad consoled.

"No, Dad! Please, I can't face it!—not Christmas!" I choked up and said goodbye.

I threw myself on the bed and cried in hug sobs. "God, this is so sad! My mother's dead, and it's Christmastime, and I'm alone. I feel like the rejected souls of society must feel, who go to rescue missions because they have no place to go for Christmas," I cried into my pillow and prayed.

Christmas. Once again the media displays its expertise in making all of us believe what they want us to believe—that Christmas is one big splurge—buying and giving and receiving bigger and better gifts than ever before.

It's a funny thing. Somehow they make us believe that everybody is happier than we are. (They got what we didn't.)

My travel agent laughed when I said—three days before Christmas—that I wanted a flight. No chance. Planes were overbooked with standbys.

By the time I called Dad again, I had cried and wallowed in self-pity, and then pulled myself out with prayer and *a plan.*

"Dad! I'll see you in two weeks! We'll celebrate Christmas then with our friends. For now, I feel God has something special for me to do this year. Dad, I may be hurting with Mom being gone, and I won't be able to be with you, but there are other singles out here who are hurting a thousand times more than I. I get so much warmth and love in life! I must get more than any other unmarried in the country! So I'll "pray in" those people who need a big Christmas dinner. And I'll give each one a gift. I'll make song sheets and play the guitar, and Bernie can sing, with background music on the tape recorder."

"Honey, I prayed you would think of something wonderful. This is more than I prayed for. I love you, lots, and I'm proud of you. I'll see you in a couple of weeks. Bye, Honey."

I called the Christian radio station where I was formerly employed. "Listen, I know it's only two days before Christmas, and I should have gotten this announcement in to you before now, but listen to this! I want to invite any single who is alone on Christmas Day to come to my house for dinner, caroling, and fireside fellowship! Will you announce it today?"

"Käaren, are you sure you want to do this? You could get a lot of kooky people and calls!" one of the staff questioned.

"Never mind! I *want* to do it!" I insisted.

"We interrupt this broadcast to bring you a special announcement: Käaren Witte is inviting any single person, who is alone in the city, to a Christmas Dinner at her home. . . ." came the message moments later.

I cooked for the next two days, making special Christmas breads with frosting and nuts, fresh fruit salads, and vegetables in seasoned sauces. I found a huge turkey at the supermarket— a real beauty.

And then my guests came—some I had met before and some were new friends. Before we ate, we sang around the table "Oh, Come, All Ye Faithful." And that's what I felt—joyful and triumphant.

I made Christmas warm and caring for over twenty people. Oh, these weren't people who were expressive, glib or colorful. . . . They even seemed to have a general understanding that no one ask why anyone else wasn't with families or loved ones. Conversation at the table was centered around the food.

By eleven o'clock that night the last person had left. The dishes were stacked on every counter in the kitchen. The living room was strewn with empty cups, glasses, cracker-and-cheese trays, cookie plates and candy dishes. Gift wrappings and ribbons lay on the floor, and candles were dripping puddles of wax.

I looked around again. I decided there was a tomorrow. Instead of cleaning up, I went to my bed and fell on it! My back was aching and my feet were killing me! But I smiled as I put my arms behind my head. What satisfaction.

It was a beautiful Christmas celebration, because this is what Christmas is at its best—giving. As it turned out, I think I received more from it than anyone else there.

A New Year's Prayer

"Jesus, help me to pursue godliness and not marriage.
It's your will that I first be a godly young woman.
Help me to nurture the same desires in my single life as I
    have for marriage: to be self-sacrificing, and to serve my
    loved ones.
Help me to encourage other people to live holy lives, as
    much as I encourage them in their social lives!
By your grace, I will not settle for anyone but your first choice.
I will relax.
Your timing is perfect.
So are your gifts.
It's like this . . .
        Mom would always give me perfect gifts—
        Like that white scarf and hat that accented my black
            coat,
        And the red purse that matched my red shoes.
She gave the right gifts. Always!
Because she knew me so well!
And, Jesus, you know me even better.
So I can trust you to give me perfect gifts, too!

Two Gathered in My Name

It was 6:30 PM. "Sandy!" I gasped, "I don't know the address of the church! We'll have to trust the Lord right on this freeway! I don't have a clue—my mind's a blank."

It was like pulling the pin, throwing the grenade, cupping my hands over my ears and waiting for the explosion.

"God will lead us," Sandy affirmed unemotionally.

I eased up considerably. (Sandy is my good friend. She's single, and she sings. Sometimes she travels with me.)

My mind went back to other incidents like this one. I would sometimes forget to take the directions or get mixed up. And usually the other person began spouting something like, "Käaren! This is so scatterbrained! This is just like you. No, we're not going to find the place. I just know it!"

But not Sandy. She said she would trust the Lord right with me. We became two hearts united in one spirit.

"You know I usually am a bit more organized than this," I continued as I drove, "but this time I didn't get the address and directions. I have asked God to forgive me for this stupid negligence here in a big, strange city."

"Dear God, bless Sandy for her faith. But please bail me out!" I prayed as we drove down the freeway.

I had been at this church a couple of years ago, but nothing looked familiar. My mind was a blank. I told Sandy, "Wait! I do remember one thing! The church was near a pie shop!"

"Oh. Okay. Ah-h-h . . . any 'leadings' to get off this freeway?" Sandy inquired, as we drove past exit after exit.

"Let's take this one. What do you think?" I said.

"Yes, I think this is it!" Sandy agreed.

"Sandy! The word Federal just popped into my mind!" I exclaimed.

"Federal, what??? Savings and Loan? Federal Reserve? Federal case?" she quizzed, never doubting, however, that

God's Holy Spirit was in control.

I was relaxed. Totally believing. And, wow! I was grateful for Sandy. For this experience was to be one of the most valuable lessons in what can be accomplished when two people stand in agreement, speak the Word, claim those promises, and believe that the Holy Spirit will lead—just like He promised He would always do!

Sandy often traveled with me and sang at the meetings. But I was seeing one of the greater blessings that God had in mind for the two of us . . . in our adventure of walking in His Spirit!

"Sandy, I think we should turn left!" I announced as we drove through the Florida night.

"So do I," she said. "Does any of this look familiar *now*, Käaren?"

"Nothing. But should we turn again or keep going straight??" I asked.

"Dear God, we sense you are leading us! We're totally dependent on you. We don't have any ideas right now!" I prayed, "In Jesus' name we stand in agreement that you will bring us to the church on time. We take authority over Satan and all his agents. You can't make us doubt! We claim the scripture, 'Lo! I am with you always!' "

"I believe we should turn!" Sandy announced.

"Right or left?"

"Right!" She said, "Oh! But you can't go over there, Käaren! You'll be in the wrong lane! We must go back around the block and pick up the turn."

As we drove around the block I yelled, "There's Federal! It's a big street!"

"Get on it!" Sandy rejoiced and laughed.

6:50 PM: "Any direction to turn off Federal??" I asked.

"No," she assured. "Does anything look familiar *NOW*?"

"Not a thing, I'll keep going."

6:55 PM: We hit a stop light. The red light seemed stuck. "Look! There's a pie shop!" Sandy shouted, "Is that the one?

Does Mother Hubbard's Pie Shop ring a bell?"

"That's it! Mother Hubbard's!" I applauded, as I looked up into the night sky and saw a steeple. "And there's the church!"

6:57 PM! I'm not sure if the parking spot we found was legal. (But when such grace was abounding, anything short of a sign, bright-yellow lines, and a six-foot-tall meter maid was open territory, I figured.) But the Lord probably did reserve it for us.

I won't put anything past the Lord.

6:59 PM: We walked in. We made the 7:00 PM meeting. Little did they know.

Please understand I'm not recommending that a Christian plan for God's supernatural intervention for every lapse in memory—but it was kind of fun this once! (And I *am* more careful now to get clear directions before starting out.)

My Father loves me and cares for me, flaws and all, and He is teaching me. . . .

Motives

"You two gals are more than welcome to stay here! See, we've just built a private entrance on this new bedroom addition. It's for guests like you! So feel welcome anytime! You can stay with us between your speaking-singing engagements or when you want to take a few vacation days!" The pastor of a local Miami church said to Sandy and myself.

Since it was impossible to find a motel, we were delighted with the gracious invitation, and later that night, at the church, we accepted the offer!

"Here we are!" we called, as we made our way over to him. "We're finished speaking and singing for a few days, so we'd like to take you up on your kind offer!"

"Oh," he said, wiping away his smile. "I, ah-h, um. I'll ah-h-h . . . have to check with Alice. She's already gone home. Well . . . ah, you can follow me. We'll ah-h-h see. . . ."

Sandy and I walked to the car. It was nearly midnight. We were getting the picture.

"Sandy! What happened to the Christian hospitality line we got this morning?" I questioned.

"He's just tired," Sandy reasoned, "I'm sure Alice will be glad for the chance to help some fellow Christians!"

Pulling into their driveway, I rolled down the window only to hear the pastor say, "Wait here, girls. I'll check with Alice."

"This is getting to be humiliating!" I said to Sandy.

Two minutes later, the pastor waved to us from the door. We went in. He smiled. She didn't.

"Ah-h-h. Um. We have our sleeping bags. We even have our own towels," I jumped in, trying to save the icy moment any way I could.

"I hope the kids won't wake you. They get up early to watch cartoons," Alice cautioned, trying to discourage our staying.

"Oh. Um . . . we must get up early anyway! We'll be up and

out of here before you know it," I filled in again.

"That's right. We must get up early. We have so much to do!" Sandy added. (She wasn't just whistling Dixie.)

"I'm burning with humiliation! How un-Christian! And I thought they were our new friends! How pathetic! We don't have to look like destitute rejects! We have some money. We don't have to be stripped of our self-respect and self-esteem, Sandy! They can't do this to us!" I cried as we lay in our sleeping bags.

"I've got it!" I continued. "We're going to teach these people a real lesson! We're going to write them a gushy thank-you note, thanking them for their wonderful love, warmth, friendship, and Christian hospitality! Then we're going to leave them a book, a record, and $40!" I continued gleefully. "Won't they feel small! Can you imagine owning this lavish, five-bedroom Goldcoast mansion . . . and acting this way? Well, we'll show them!"

"Yeah!" Sandy cheered and laughed. "This'll cream 'em!"

With our dignity somewhat restored, we slept fast and slipped away in the pre-dawn Miami morning . . . without even using their bathroom.

At the local Lums Restaurant, we changed clothes, washed, and brushed our teeth.

The following Sunday at the church, we saw them pushing their way through the crowded foyer to get to us.

"Sandy! Käaren! Wait!" Alice began as she took our arms, "You have no idea how the Lord used you two. . . . When you came over, I just couldn't face any more company—we had no money. We may look well off, but we are deeply in debt. In fact, that day I didn't know what Bill was going to use for gas money! We had zero balance in our checking account—and then we woke up, and found the money you gave us!"

"How gracious and Christian you young ladies were. Just like the Bible says . . . you did it. When others did you wrong . . . you hardly noticed. You just went on loving us and seeing us as *we should be*," the pastor chimed in, choking a bit.

We forced smiles. We didn't look at each other. We pushed

out some words, and edged for the door.

"Ah-h...look who's doing the cringing and the crawling now...." I gulped to Sandy.

Wrong motives. They always backfire. But somehow God used them. For all of us.

What Happens When Women Pray (about fat)

Amazing! That's how I'd describe what happened.

For years, my church formed small spiritual-growth groups. Clusters of people studied the Bible, memorized scripture, prayed and pulled for one another.

Since there were several of us who fought fat I suggested starting a "No Growth Group". (Give us this day our daily bread. But hold the mayo.)

Together, another friend and myself began praying for the various gospel blimps in the kingdom as well as for those, like myself, who wore a size 12 but should wear a ten.

(I want you to know, I've come a long way. At one time, I thought a pie or a cake were individual servings. I never met a potato I didn't like. I'd look at a cookie and wonder if I should swallow it or apply it directly to my hips. My view was: until you crush a moped or the government gives you your own zip code, don't sweat it.)

But now, I didn't want to be speaking to people about the fruit of the Spirit, which includes self-control, while having un-controlled Sara Lee attacks, being so unfit I'd be huffing and ex-hausted from just dialing long distance or chewing gum.

One of the hardest things for people to change is their eat-ing habits. But one of the greatest claims of Jesus Christ is that we can do *all things* through Him. And that includes controlling our food intake.

So, my friend and I made a list of those saints who obviously needed to lose. We never even told them we were praying for them. (So what are you supposed to say, "I'm praying for your fat, friend"?)

Suddenly, one gal on the list decreased in size. Noticeably. "Sue-Marie! Did you lose weight?? You have!!" I discreetly, but excitedly asked.

"Yes! I've lost over forty pounds, Käaren. I've got just another 80 to go!" she beamed.

"Oh, Sue-Marie, I've never told you, but another friend and I have formed a "No Growth Group!" We've been praying for you!"

"Oh, Käaren, the Lord *is* helping me to do this difficult thing. I never had been able to lose weight. But I have made this commitment. I was so convicted about being overweight. I just had to quit bringing shame to the Temple of the Holy Spirit—my body. So Jesus Christ and I are doing it together. I know I will make my weight goal with His power," she confirmed.

A week later, I spotted Dorothy. She had shed thirty pounds and reached her ideal weight. She was giving God the glory because "He heals all our diseases."

Then there were others—Jim, Beth, Alan. . . .

And Carol—I hadn't seen Carol for six months, but I had heard this single young woman—a real doll with a five-hundred-watt smile—brought her 5'2", former 220-pound frame down to a petite 120!

I stared. I hugged her. I cried, "Carol! This is making a believer out of me!"

"It's a miracle—it proves Jesus Christ's words. Doesn't it? He means what He says. We can do *anything* through Him—tough, impossible things," she softly assured me.

I lost fifteen pounds when I simply stopped eating sugar and started a little jogging. But it's an every day commitment. And every day I get on my knees and say, "With your help, Jesus, I will weigh what I should."

Jesus Christ died on a cross two thousand years ago for our sins and our sicknesses. If a weight-problem fits into either category for us, it's included in that sacrifice.

Together we can do it. We're believers.

Attractiveness

Sometimes I question my "desirability." Am I physically appealing? Am I attractive?

I get pats on the back and compliments from the people in my church, my family, and people in my audiences—married ladies, and their mates, singles, grandmothers and granddads, kids and teens—but rarely from a special man! That one-in-all-the-world-who-chose-me-type of man. (You understand. I just know you do.)

But, every once in a while, one of those rare individuals comes into my life—be it ever so brief. It's a reminder....

Maybe it happens at a conference, or a TV station, or while speaking at a church like the time in Pittsburgh.

At this church, I spoke and shared stories from my first book, *Angels in Faded Jeans.* I told these dear people that God was still in the miracle business and how He had allowed me—this small-town girl from Worthington, Minnesota, to experience some of them.

The pastor was young—and single. Manly. A leader. Warm. Articulate. He thought I was "special." And he kept saying so! It made even me gun-shy. I could hardly talk above a whisper on a one-to-one! (He was that powerfully charming!)

After I left, he called and wrote occasionally. He said nice things—about me!

But, I was reminded that I'm not accepted or rejected on the basis of what someone says about me.

I used to think if I didn't have a date, I was rejected. On the other hand, just because someone compliments me doesn't mean I have to fall in love with him!

So, from this dynamic pastor, though it was a tough assignment, I took the compliments in stride, with a simple, "Thank you!" I knew he was only being kind and thoughtful as a Christian gentleman.

Nice people say nice things. What's in the heart comes out of the mouth.

Words, actions, and attitudes may or may not reveal the truth about us. But it will reveal what's in someone's heart.

Now isn't that freeing?

God's Chipping Away (at anything that doesn't resemble His Son)

I was bone tired. Spent. No yuks or giggles left. I had spoken three times in one day.

I stayed with a family overnight. They "needed" me to listen (at 10:30 PM) to what they majored in at the U of Wisconsin in 1959. There were the endless photo albums and five, count them, *five* cartridges of slides. Then there was the detailed account of their son's sixth-grade lead (in deadly detail) in "A Christmas Carol."

I had prayed the same prayer for years: "Please, God. Couldn't some host say, 'Käaren, we want to minister to *you*. We want to bless and encourage you. What are your needs? Your heart cries? Your interests? We want to *serve you*.' "

But nobody ever did.

Then the words of a pastor changed me: "Käaren, seek His face! Not His hand! Bless God! Don't always ask Him to serve you. Serve Him!"

Yes, there it was—I saw the lesson. I'd been using and *abusing* God. I was the same as others—oozing with needs. Pathetically needy. But, I was making God my celestial robot. My divine, private genie. "Do this! Arrange that! Prosper me! Bless me!" Demands. Cries.

When did I bless Jesus?

(Do you get the idea that my whole life—every word and every action—has *grace* written across it? Grace heaped upon grace.)

It does.

Now, That's What I Call Fun

There was a "Fun Run" for runners around the Minneapolis Lakes. I went to watch.

The faces expressed anguish. Twisted, frowning. Tortured. (Some fun.)

I began jogging this year. Nothing marathon, mind you. But enough to feel good.

While watching the runners, I thought, "Fun to me means imagination and creativity! A party! Children! Music! Costumes! Candy, gum, and prizes for the kids!"

So I put the idea into action. Every day, I now put on one of *my costumes* especially designed for running! And I really have a "fun run!" I have music playing via a little recorder or small radio. And in my Superman outfit, or my White Rabbit outfit or my slightly fuzzy Brown Bear costume, or my Black Mouse costume, complete with long tail—I *run* around the lakes! I wave to passers-by and hand out little treats to the children, and gospel tracts.

Sometimes people ask me to have my picture taken with them. I break stride and pose. (Twice, in my bear costume, I was asked if I give bear hugs.)

Once I handed a lady on a lakeside bench a gospel tract and a stick of gum while wearing my floppy-eared rabbit costume.

"Leave it to the Christian to find creative ways to get the Good News out! Praise the Lord!" she called to me, laughing and applauding.

As I continued to run, Evie was singing "The Lord makes me happy ... He gives me the best in every day. ..." on KTIS radio. (It's just like the Lord to make the run in life—fun.)

He is the author of creativity. He has a great track record for imagination and originality. (Planets, the universe— all of us so dramatically different.) And He said that we could be all that He is just for the asking!

So, would you put anything past the Lord in your life?

Spring 1981

The Cost

I get weary of speakers and writers trying to persuade us that following Jesus Christ means high-rise luxury living and six-figure incomes, and marriage and a family on schedule.

When young women sit on my living room couch, and they want to be born into the glorious kingdom of God, I tell them to consider *the cost.*

"Don't give your life to Jesus Christ unless you are ready to be His follower *anywhere* and under any conditions."

Jesus' very words are recorded in the fourteenth chapter of Luke: "And no one can be my disciple who does not carry his own cross and follow me. But *don't begin* until you *count the cost.* . . . So no one can become my disciple unless he first sits down and counts his blessings—and then *renounces them all for me.*" (TLB)

Following Christ may cost you boyfriends, a husband, a family—safety, and comfort. There are no rough estimates. The cost is high.

A man once said to me, "Käaren, I wouldn't live like you have to live and pay the awful price you are demanded to pay as a Christian and a single . . . not for a million dollars."

I said, "Neither would I."

I was convinced my relatives, and the people in my church thought: "How pathetic—Käaren isn't married. She must not make the grade with men. Something's wrong with her. She must be doing something wrong."

Now I know they believe, because I do, that I am called to be single—at least, for now. And, maybe, forever. Because God needs me to be His follower on an assignment that calls for singleness.

Being a Christian means paying whatever price is necessary. It demands the strongest, bravest, and most committed men and women.

November 1981

Winter Morning

I wanted to stay under the electric blanket (turned up to ten). It's winter now in Minnesota—you know, a winter wonderland?

Instead, I made orange spice tea, and punched in an Evie tape. I scanned the Minneapolis paper, then answered ten reader's letters from the stack.

I read from Phillipians, weighed myself, even thought about calling the White House (the number is 202-456-1414.) Prayed for Dad, ate two bran muffins—(wished I had eaten one.) Saw a jogger go by—felt guilty about not running. (Low guilt threshold.) Flicked on Phil Donahue, wondering about the subject and guest. Called Cheryl at work. She has a cold. (Her prayer request was for new boots—and a husband).

I walked to the co-op—filled and weighed a baggie full of walnuts. Thought maybe I'd bake. I wanted to go to lunch with my mom, and I cried because I could never do it again. Wrote a thank-you note to my pastor's wife. (Always thought I wanted to be one!)

Reviewing the routine events of my casual day, I thought about how God accepts us as the ordinary, routine-conscious people that we are.

But, He deserves more than my casual approach to Him. Doesn't He? He is NOT the "Big Guy in the Sky" or the "Man Upstairs." He is the God of the universe. He demands ultimate respect. And that's rare in a world where nothing seems sacred, and irreverence is funny and marketable.

"Dear God, Let these words about who you are be vocabulary turned into behavior." I prayed, "Let Your awesomeness turn into a healthy fear. For this is the beginning of wisdom. And that means purity and godliness for my life. A strength against temptation and sin."

I must realize *who this God is* when I step into His presence.

I must bow down and know the power of His name. (*Now* how could I ever turn *grace* into a green light for the flesh?)

I've put the whole idea of the majesty, power, and glory of Almighty God into the question: *"Is God getting out of my life what He had His Son Jesus Christ pay for?"*

A Closing Letter to My Friends
Dear Friends:

Thank you for living through with me some of my "great leaps." So, some of them didn't seem so "great"—just look at how far I've come!

Let me leave you with two ways to a fulfilled, purposeful life—a life that will bring glory to our great God!

BELIEVE YOU CAN DO IT! Believe in success for yourself and for others. Make a commitment to that cause. By building self-esteem in yourself and others, you glorify God. Achievement may be learning to live creatively with a handicap, overcoming a stubborn habit, or rebuilding your life after a crisis, death, separation, loss, or divorce. Or, it may be starting out toward a new goal, a dream, a new career . . . and it will happen! Because Jesus Christ said with Him ALL THINGS are possible! No exceptions. Claim it. Stake your life on it!

BELIEVE IN GRACE! So many people are bitter and resentful. They think they haven't gotten what they deserve in life, and feel that others have. But when we open the Scriptures, we become eternally grateful. We didn't get *what we really deserved*!

An interviewer once asked what my goal in life was: Best-selling books, TV programs, large audiences?

I can honestly say, if no one had ever heard of me, and I lived in discomfort, sorrow and pain . . . I would still have a reason to be brave. Life here is short—but, eternity isn't. Jesus says one day at a time is all that matters.

Thank you, again, dear friends, for allowing me to share myself with you.

And to you, Mom . . . beyond the sunset in the glorious promised presence of Jesus Christ . . . I told them. I told them the best I could. Jesus Christ is the reason to live and the reason to die.

I always love hearing from my readers. You may write to me in care of the publisher, 6820 Auto Club Road, Minneapolis, Minnesota 55438.

Big, incredible blessings on you, In Jesus' Name!

Love always, I promise,

Käaren Witte

P.S. Thank you for being part of my family. I'm so glad we're "related!" If you've never been born-again, born into the family of God, wouldn't you do it right now? Salvation through Jesus Christ is yours just for the asking.

Come to Christ: "Him that cometh to me I will in no wise cast out" (John 6:37).

Accept Christ: "As many as received him, to them gave he power to become the sons of God, even to them that believe on his name" (John 1:1, 2).

Confess Christ: "If thou shalt confess with thy mouth the Lord Jesus, and shalt believe in thine heart that God hath raised him from the dead, thou shalt be saved" (Romans 10:9).

This salvation was provided for us:

Because we were guilty: "By one man sin entered into the world, and death by sin; and so death passed upon all men, for that all have sinned" (Romans 5:12).

Because of the love of God: "Herein is love, not that we loved God, but that He loved us, and sent His Son to be the propitiation for our sins" (1 John 4:10).

Because of the death of Christ: "Christ died for our sins according to the scriptures . . . he was buried, and . . . he rose again the third day according to the scriptures" (1 Cor. 15:3, 4). "The Lord hath laid on him the iniquity of us all" (Isaiah 53:6).

Settle this question once and for all, dear friends. And let me hear of your decision to follow and be committed to our wonderful Jesus Christ.

And I'll see you . . . when we all get home.